# LISTEN TO ME AND
# COLLEGE WILL BE EASY

# LISTEN TO ME AND COLLEGE WILL BE EASY

A Handbook on How to
Make College Work for You

L.M. BEDELL

ISBN: 978-0-615-58737-0
Library of Congress Control Number: 2012902330

Printed in the United States of America
By BookLogix
Alpharetta, Georgia

10 9 8 7 6 5 4 3 2                    0 4 1 9 1 3

∞This paper meets the requirements of ANSI/NISO
Z39.48-1992 (Permanence of Paper)

Designers: Lance Moore and Jasmine Charleston

This book is dedicated to Mac Bedell.

*Dad,*

*I know you are in heaven reading my book, with a Coca-Cola in your hand.*

*Also dedicated to everyone who believed in me when I didn't believe in myself. My college years weren't the easiest but they have made me the person that I am today. I have many lasting and unforgettable memories that I will carry with me. This is not just a thank you note for my mom and dad, but a token of appreciation for my family, friends, colleagues, teachers and professors, and everyone who made an ambitious girl from Decatur, Georgia become a driven young lady that will grace the entire world.*

# A NOTE TO THE READER:

I am so glad that you have a copy of this handbook. I promise that it's not your ordinary boring book that rambles on and on about things that you don't care to hear about. It won't confuse you with big words that you have to search for in the dictionary. I understand that college students have a tremendous workload and don't need to be bogged down with another task of trying to read information that's hard to grasp. That's why this book is more of a guide to help you have the best four years of your life. I've been through the holes and cracks of a college education, now this is my opportunity to help you while you transition into college life and beyond. I will cover everything from picking the right professors to how to dress on a job interview. I promise that you are in for a treat! So grab your favorite beverage and get a head start on your next four years.

Thanks so much,

L.M. Bedell

# CONTENTS

# PRE-COLLEGE CHECKLIST

**While you are in high school, here is a list of things you should keep in mind...**

- Keep a clean behavior and academic record...college acceptance officials look at this.

- Take at least two college preparatory courses. Preparation is the key to success!

- When writing papers, take it very seriously...you will be writing extensively at the college level.

- Learn how to take good notes and study.

- Read your textbooks...this will come in handy at the next level.

- Earn the highest grade point average (GPA) possible...this will look good on your college application.

- Study thoroughly for the ACT (American College Testing Assessment) and SAT (Scholastic Aptitude Test) and get the highest scores possible. Not only will this look good on your college application, but it can help you win scholarships.

$$$$$$$$$$

- Research five colleges based on: what major you want to declare, ACT/SAT scores, location, cost, scholarships available, campus life, size, chances of getting accepted, and job placement rates.

- Apply to all five schools. If you are not accepted to two of them, you will still have three to choose from.

- Research scholarships and different schools that offer certain scholarships. You may be able to receive a scholarship simply because you are a minority, want to study environmental science, etc.

- Is your FAFSA (Free Application for Federal Student Aid) complete? Don't miss out on the opportunity to receive *free money!*

- Take a career personality test such as the Myers-Briggs Type Indicator (MBTI).

- Read my book before starting college. ☺

# WHY SHOULD YOU GET A COLLEGE DEGREE?

According to the College Board[1], college enables you to...

- Expand your knowledge and skills
- Express your thoughts clearly in speech and in writing
- Grasp abstract concepts and theories
- Increase your understanding of the world and your community

## WHAT DOES THIS MEAN FOR YOU?

*More Job Opportunities*: The world is changing rapidly. More and more jobs require education beyond high school. College graduates have more jobs to choose from than those who don't pursue education beyond high school.

*Earn More Money*: A person who goes to college usually earns more than a person who doesn't. This information is based on the US Census Bureau's

---

[1] www.collegeboard.com

2008 median earnings for full-time workers at least twenty-five years old.

Annual earnings, based on degree, are:

    High school diploma, $33,801

    Associate degree, $42,046

    Bachelor's degree, $55,656

    Master's degree, $67,337

    Professional degrees, $100,000+

# DON'T DOUBT YOURSELF

The College Board lists five excuses students give for not wanting to attend college...

1. *I can't afford it.*

Most students get financial aid to help pay for college, and most aid is based on need. This means that the less money you have, the more aid you might get.

2. *Nobody in my family has ever gone.*

Being first can be hard. For instance, you may have to explain to your family why college is important to you. On the other hand, being first is likely to be a source of pride for you and for your family.

3. *I don't know what I want to do with my life.*

Join the crowd. Thousands of college freshmen haven't decided on a major or career. College gives you the opportunity to learn more about what's out there. You'll be exposed to a variety of academic subjects, people, and new perspectives.

4. *College is too hard for me.*

Most students think college will be too hard for them. Keep in mind, all colleges offer tutoring and student support. As confident as some students seem, no one goes to college knowing everything—if they did, why would they go?

5. *I just won't fit in.*

Most colleges have students from many backgrounds. To get an idea of what to expect, explore colleges through www.collegeboard.com or better yet, visit the campus. Be sure to ask around about the make-up of the student body, and if they have clubs and activities that you're interested in joining.

# CHAPTER | 1

# FRESHMAN YEAR

*I think of a hero as someone who understands the degree of responsibility that comes with his freedom.*

– Bob Dylan

On the first day in a higher learning institute, you may be nervous, scared, and not know which direction to turn. I went to a huge university that enrolls over 30,000 students a year so I was feeling all of those emotions. I put the "s" in scared and the "n" in nervous. College can be a frightening situation to step into because it's a new experience that you are unsure about. Questions like *Will I be able to make new friends? What if I have an emergency? What if I run out of money? and What if I don't do well?* will pop in your head at some point but you can't be overcome by them. You must understand that these questions will pop in your head when you are a sophomore, junior, and a senior. The funny thing about college is that these questions will never disappear, but they will be given less attention with good planning and constructive advice. It's

1

perfectly natural for you to be worried about how you will do your first year in school, but I believe in you and greatness is on its way.

REMEMBER: Freshman year will probably be the most fun you will have in college.

As a freshman, many students don't work a part-time job so they have lots of time on their hand. What is good and bad about having too much time on your hands...

**Good:**

This is the time to meet a lot of other students while hanging around campus and the dorms. In fact, about half of the people you will meet in college will be those you meet during your freshman year. Since you and your friends have a lot of time, you should go shopping, challenge each other in sports, and dine at the nearest inexpensive restaurants. You should learn about their heritage and ask questions about their family, while enlightening them about your own. I am personally asking you to take full advantage of the ample amount of time you'll have to get to know and enjoy your friends, because that same time will begin to fade as you progress throughout your college career.

## Bad:

Having lots of time on your hands can also put you in uncompromising situations. This time can lead many to smoking, drinking, and excessive partying, which jeopardizes the ultimate reason why you are in college—*to receive a quality education.* You are better than that and I don't want you to let one mistake be the reason why you are kicked out of school. These activities cause students to neglect studying and completing their schoolwork, which will reflect in their grades. I often hear that only the "cool kids" drink and smoke because it's the thing to do. I often reply "those students will not be cool when they have to drop out of school only to end up working at a fast food joint for the rest of their lives." I'm not trying to be your mother, father, grandmother, or grandfather, but I don't want you to make some of the mistakes that some of my friends did. I'm saddened by the fact that some of my friends that were freshman when I was one did not graduate from college with me because of poor choices and bad decisions. Think about what I just said and create positive memories with your spare time.

## Freshman Orientation

Although most people consider orientations as boring, time-consuming, and redundant, your freshman orientation will be an introduction to your new school. If you have to attend one orientation in your life, freshman orientation will probably be the most important one. As a freshman, you are like a newborn transitioning from your mother to the world. For this reason, attending this orientation will give you a glimpse into the world of college. It will tell you about all the resources that are available to you as a student. Just go and learn as much as possible so I will not have to keep writing about freshman orientation. LOL

## Picking Classes and Professors

Having a successful freshman year determines the fate of your next three years. It's important to obtain a high grade point average because it's easy for it to fall but hard to raise it back up. If you have a GPA of less than 2.5, raising it will be like climbing Mount Everest—it will be tedious, long and hard. This is why you must do well in your first year classes. Thus, the type of classes you choose and the professors who teach those classes are paramount.

First, pick easy classes during your freshman year. Choose lower level courses, which usually begin with a one or two. Courses starting with a 3 or 4 and higher are upper division courses that demand a lot of work to be successful in them. Load your schedule with art, music, history, and political science classes. These classes will not be difficult, but actually fun and informative. If you are attending a big college/university, these types of classes will consist of lots of students. The more students in a class equate to professors giving multiple choice tests instead of essay based exams.

**TIP:** Not only should you attend EVERY class, but sit in the front. The closer you are to the professor, the closer you are to knowledge.

To do well in these courses, you have to read your text books, listen in class, and take good notes. If you do these things, you will do very well.

Never pick difficult classes during freshman year. You should avoid certain science courses such as biology and chemistry because they will require you to learn lots of information and studying for them will be in-depth and demanding. In such courses, you will learn a slew of terminologies and formulas that will consume a lot of your time in grasping the information. I am not doubting your ability to do well in difficult classes, but I think these courses should be taken when you have learned how to prepare and study for college exams (which is usually learned after your first year in college). Also, many students take a math course during their first year. If you're like me and not a mathematical genius, then working out college algebra or its equivalence will take much effort.

Don't stress...

The college that you are attending will most likely have math tutors in the math department that will be glad to assist you. In fact, they are getting paid to assist students who have trouble in their math courses. Lots of students are intimidated by math courses and their performance reflects the fear they have of the subject. I took college algebra during my first year and I received a B+. I received that grade thanks to the help of my math tutor. I was extremely worried that I wouldn't do well in the class but I passed with flying colors.

Accordingly, picking good professors is just as important as knowing what classes to take. So what is a good professor? A good professor teaches as well as listens to his/her students. He or she is sensitive to the needs of the students because everyone does not learn similarly or at the same pace. When you arrive on campus, you will be given a counselor or advisor that will help you transition into college life. During your advisement meetings, ask your advisor what professor you should take for certain classes. Chances are that your counselor or advisor may know many of the professors and can recommend what professors to take or not to take. Also, go to different departments (such as Math, Science, Sociology, Political science, etc) and ask around about different professors and classes. These departments are your direct connection to professors because their offices are going to be located within them. This would be a good way to start your freshman year on the right foot by visiting your prospective instructors. In fact, this would help you build a relationship with him/her and leave a first impression that your professor won't forget. Lastly, websites such as *ratemyprofessor.com* and *pickaprof.com* allow you to view past student's experiences with professors. These websites also show how the professors have graded students. Picking professors is an important task that will be easier as you progress in college.

REMEMBER: As you take classes, you can then ask your professors about their colleagues, which will also help you to choose prospective professors. You've got to get your foot in the door, but when you do; your classes will be particularly manageable.

**Buying Books**

Okay; you have picked your classes and professors, now you have the task of buying the books that you will need to complete the classes.

First, when you find out who your professors will be, email them and ask what books you will need for class. Many students will go to the bookstore and buy books according to what the store has listed. However, the professor may not require you to have that book or they may prefer another book. If this happens, you will have to go through the hassle of returning the book and buying something else. Believe me, returning books that you do not need can be aggravating. You have a short amount of time to return them for a full refund and books with shrink-wraps must be returned in their original packaging. Also, during the first week of classes, the bookstore is hectic and overcrowded. To avoid the frustration of you becoming impatient, *email your professors and ask them the exact book/s you will need for class*. This will allow you to shop around for the best prices and avoid long lines at the college's bookstore. I promise you that doing this will make your life so much easier.

REMEMBER: Life is going to be chaotic during your first couple of weeks as a freshman, so make your life less stressful by obtaining your books effectively and efficiently.

You can get lucky and get books from students who have already taken the class. If you reside in a dorm, ask other students what classes they have completed. You will find out if they have taken the classes that you will take and they may let you borrow the books that they don't need anymore. While on campus, ask around and find out if other students have books that they are no longer using. If they let you borrow a book or two, make sure to thank them and let them know how you are doing in the class. This would also be a great opportunity for you to ask them any questions you may have about the class. Here is a list of possible questions to ask a student who has completed a class that you are about to take…

1. Did the class require lots of reading and outside research?

2. About how many term papers did you have to write?

3. Did the professor lecture with or without PowerPoint slides? (This matters because if the professor lectures with power point slides, he/she may make them available to you. You will be able to print them and write important notes on them during class)

4. What did the exams consist of? Multiple choices, short answer, essay, or a combination of all three?

5. Did the professor thoroughly review for exams or did students have to rely on study groups as a review? (This matters because if a professor gives a review session before a test, the most important/relevant information will be discussed.)

6. What did you most like about the class?

7.   What did you least like about the class?

8.   Did you ever consider dropping the class because of its difficulty or lack thereof?

9.   If you still have notes from the class, can I take a look at them?

10.  Would you recommend the class to other students?

## That Forgotten Syllabus

In every class you take while in college, you will receive a syllabus that outlines the course objectives/goals, reading material, assignments, grading scale, and professor's office hours & contact information.

*Who cares about a syllabus, it's just a couple sheets of paper?*

As insignificant as a syllabus might sound, it plays a critical role in you becoming successful in the course. You will be **aware** of everything that will occur during the duration of the semester, for example...

1.   The books your professor will use

2.   The dates when you will take an exam and how many exams will be given

3.   What material will be covered on an exam

4.   What days class will be cancelled

5. When research papers are due and what they should cover

6. Your professor's grading scale

7. If extra credit will be given or accepted

8. How many absences you are allowed before they begin to affect your grade

9. General expectations

10. The college or university's no cheating policy—You will hear this a lot...**DON'T CHEAT.** *And of course, I did not have to tell you that—you already know it!*

REMEMBER: Your syllabi are given for the purpose of equipping you with the tools you need to successfully complete a course. Don't do yourself a disservice by not reading it or not keeping up with important assignments and dates.

**Real Life Scenarios**

*Throughout high school, Clay never read his syllabi. When he began college and started to take classes that required lots of reading and assignments, he continued not to read his syllabi. Consequently, Clay never studied for a pop quiz that was listed on his syllabus and not mentioned by the professor. The quiz was worth 10 percent (or one point) of his final grade. He failed the quiz and that ultimately was the difference in him receiving a C instead of the B he could have gotten.*

## That Forgotten Catalog

Similar to your syllabi, every major offered will have a catalog. This catalog outlines the classes, internships, and other requirements needed in order to successfully complete the major in question. From personal experience, most people never crack open their major's catalog. However, this catalog will ensure that you stay on track by taking the right classes in order to graduate on time. You don't want to arrive at your senior year and realize that you took a couple courses that don't apply to your major. If this happens, you will have to take additional courses, which will extend your time in college and the money that you will have to pay. This situation can be totally preventable by using your catalog as a reference when picking which classes to take.

## Residing On Campus vs. Residing Off Campus

I never resided on campus and I regret not doing so. Most of my friends and the people that I came in contact with all had resided on campus during their freshman year. Just hearing all of their recollections and stories about how much fun they had, I wish that I would have stayed on campus. I feel as though I missed out on a vital part of my college experience. Even though I enjoyed my overall experience, I always wonder what freshman year would have been like if I stayed on campus. If I could go back and start college over again, I would definitely reside on campus. The networking and connections you will make while living on campus are irreplaceable.

## *This is what I found out about students who never stay on campus*

Commuter colleges and those with few students living on campus are believed to lower students' integration by...

1.   Making it easier for students to become involved in competing social roles.

2.   Limiting access to faculty outside the classroom.

3.   Decreasing peer and faculty socialization to traditional academic norms and values.[1]

Here are some challenges I faced while residing off campus

1.   While commuting downtown, I often faced a traffic dilemma. I was late to class a few times because of traffic.

---

[1] Michael Delucchi. "Academic Performance in College Town." *Education*, (1993): 114.1.

2.    Many group study sessions were held on campus and I was not on campus to be a part of them.

3.    Likewise, many events were held on campus later in the evening and it was not feasible to drive back downtown to attend them.

4.    I had many research assignments that were not easy to complete because my job and residence did not allow much flexibility to spend free time in the library.

5.    Lack of parking and expensive parking.

6.    I always felt left out. ☹

### *If you don't stay on campus, it's not all that bad*

Studies have shown that a student's GPA is influenced by residence type. Commuter students have GPAs .19 grade points higher than residents in the student community[2]. This could be due to excessive partying, alcohol use, and the pressure not to attend class that is often associated with dormitories.

It's not the end of the world if you don't reside on campus. Get involved with student organizations and study abroad, which I will be discussing in the sophomore and junior year sections of this book. I

---

[2] Michael Delucchi, "Academic Performance in College Town."

met students who stayed on campus and didn't enjoy college because they weren't involved in any campus activities. College is going to be what you make it.

TIP: If you stay off campus, don't become just a commuter student who goes to class and goes home.
GET INVOLVED, MEET PEOPLE, HAVE FUN!

### You Are an Asset

Currently, your most important asset is being a student. You are marketable because businesses/companies set prices that will drive your spending behavior.

Think about it...

Restaurants, clothing stores, convenience stores, clubs, movie theaters, museums, arenas/stadiums, recreational centers, gyms, dry cleaners, car and health insurance plans all offer some type of student discount. Use these to your advantage because **you can save money!**

### Social Life

College is a place for you to develop your social life; however this should not be placed before academia. While pursuing your education, you should have fun, make friends, gain different experiences, party responsibly, and grow into a young adult. However, everything should be done in moderation because too much of anything is not good for you.

I understand that college is a place for you to find yourself and explore new heights so here are a few pointers on balancing social life with your academics.

- Before hanging out at a party or with friends, make sure that you have completed any readings or assignments required of you.

- Don't stay out partying the night before an exam. The night before the exam, you should be studying/revisiting material you have learned.

- If you party, do so on the weekends or on nights when you don't have class the next day; this will eliminate you missing classes.

- At parties be conscientious of your actions. You don't want to have a night that scars the rest of your life. Don't get drunk because someone could take advantage of you. Carry your cup of punch around with you so that no one can slip anything in it.

- Meet and mingle with as many people as possible. Remember your network is your net worth.

- Also travel with a group of friends at night. This will reduce your chances of becoming a victim of crime.

- Attend events and lectures held on campus. This will make you a whole student rather than someone who just goes to class then back home or to their room.

- When dating, understand that both of you are young and break-ups do occur. You don't want a failed relationship to cause you to slack on your studies. On the contrary, you don't want to become so wrapped up in a person that you slack on your studies.

- Even though you are in college, keep close contact with your family and long time friends. These people will be there for you in the time of need.

REMEMBER: Your academics come first and everything else is secondary.

## The Skinny on the Freshman 15

Before                                    After

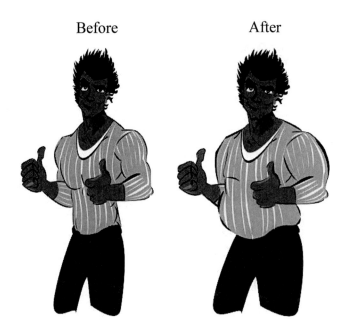

I understand that being a student, having a job, and joining different organizations can be time consuming. Due to time restraints, it may be easier to pick up fast food and eat it on the go. However, it's important that you find time to eat healthy foods and exercise. Doing this will make you feel better and give you energy to do things that you enjoy doing. You may not always feel like exercising, but it will release endorphins that reduce stress and remove toxins from your body.

Here's a couple of tips on eating healthy and exercising...

- Do not eat out at fast food restaurants every day. Try to limit eating out at fast food joints to once or twice a week at the most. If you must eat out, try to do so at an inexpensive sit-down restaurant for a nutritious meal.

- Even though you may hear horror stories about cafeteria food, eat at your school's cafeteria. Your meal plan will buy this food and it will be a lot healthier than eating off campus.

- Try not to eat after 9 p.m. Your metabolism slows down at night and it's harder to break down fat during this time frame. Eating a huge meal only to go to bed thirty minutes later is not a smart idea.

- Eat as many salads and green vegetables as possible. Even if it's only once or twice a week, your body needs it.

- Try to limit the amount of sugar (candy and sodas), fried foods, pizza, and red meat that you consume. Put those sodas down and drink water instead.

- Go grocery shopping so that you can cook/make your own food. You will be able to pick up and read the amount of calories, sodium, and fat content in what you are eating.

- Cook at least twice a week and make enough so that you can have leftovers for the next night. This will save you money, money, money, and more money.

- If you don't have time to cook, make time. There are thousands of thirty minute meal recipes that will make cooking convenient as well as healthy.

- Get mom and grand mom to make you dinner occasionally.

- WORK OUT at least three times a week. You can work out with friends in the recreation center (if there's one). Also, many colleges offer fitness classes that are FREE (well the fees were calculated in your tuition).

## Getting some Zzzzzzzzzzzzzzzzzzz's

- Students should get nine hours of sleep each night. For some, this number is a stretch so try to get at least seven hours of sleep.

- Properly resting improves brain function, which will help when you are cramming for an exam.

- You also will wake up in the morning feeling refreshed so you won't sleep through your professor's lectures.

- Rest so that you won't burn out or get sick during the semester—a healthy you equals good grades.

- Rhetorical question: How can you have fun if you're always tired? Take care of your body by giving it all the rest it needs.

### Deeper Look at Me

*A Publix supermarket was next to my job so I shopped there frequently. It was there where I found out about Publix Apron's Simple Meals. They are nutritious and inexpensive to make. You can even feed your roommates because the recipe feeds about six people! Visit* www.publix.com *for more information on Simple Recipes.*

### Do The Math....

Eating out is not only unhealthy but it is EXPENSIVE. Imagine if you ate out twice a day for five days a week. If each meal was at least $6, you would spend $60 a week and $240 a month on eating out twice a day. This doesn't include your snacks and weekend meals.

*Rather go to bed supperless, than rise in debt.*

*– Benjamin Franklin*

Do You Really Need Those Credit Cards???

**Ringing the Alarm on Credit Card Debt:**

According to *USA Today*[3]...

1.   As college costs soar, students are charging more educational expenses to plastic causing an alarming increase in credit card debt.

2.   The higher the grade level, the higher the debt according to Sallie Mae. In 2008, seniors with at least one credit card graduated with an average of $4,138 debt as compared to freshmen with an average of $2,038 debt.

Here are some college credit card debt statistics[4]...

1.   78 percent of college students have at least one credit card.

2.   32 percent of college students have at least four credit cards.

3.   On average, students have nearly three credit cards.

---

[3] Kathy Chu. *USA Today*. 2009
[4] http://www.collegestudentcreditcard.com/articles6.html

This is worth mentioning-pertinent information provided by Bloomberg[5]...

1.    "Credit card debt racked up during college is forcing more and more young people to drop out of school, change career plans, and file bankruptcy." - Rep Louise Slaughter

2.    Putting a minimum payment of $50 every month toward a $1,500 balance on a credit card with a 22 percent interest rate would take about four years to pay off.

Credit cards are sleek, easy to carry, and attractive to struggling college students. Hence, don't succumb to the pressure of having them. If you don't use them wisely, they will put you in serious debt due to strikingly high interest rates that come along with the card. I don't recommend credit cards but if you must have one, **only have one**. A credit card should not be used leisurely but for emergencies only.

**TIP**: Check with your financial aid office to see if you qualify for work-study. This would allow you to work a flexible schedule, usually on campus while earning a steady income.

---

[5] http://bloomberg.com

What are emergencies?

1.  Notification that you have to pay for your books or a portion of your tuition because there is a problem with your financial aid.

2.  You experience an unexpected problem with your car and it needs immediate repair.

3.  You get sick and need to pay for your prescription medicine.

4.  You have no money and need to buy groceries from the grocery store.

These emergencies **do not** include...

1.  You see clothes at the mall and feel that you have to buy them.

2.  Your friends invite you to an expensive restaurant and you decide to pay for your meal with your credit card.

3.   You see the latest iPod at Best Buy and feel that you have to buy it.

4.   You are having a group of friends over and want to order pizza and drinks from a local pizza parlor.

5.   You are going on a road trip and plan to use your credit card as a gas and expenses card.

REMEMBER: Credit card companies are aggressive. They will use several tactics to get you to sign up for a credit card, like offering free pizza or giving away free prizes on campus. Use your best judgment because whatever you spend on credit cards, YOU will have to pay back. You may not have money to buy expensive clothes and accessories, but keep striving to finish college. Your hard work will eventually pay off.

*The only man who never makes a mistake is the man who never does anything.*

– Theodore Roosevelt

# CHAPTER 2

# ONE YEAR DOWN...
# SOPHOMORE YEAR

*Sophomore means Wisdom...*

*What is the meaning of wisdom?*
*n. 1a. wisdom wise; good judgment 2. Knowledge*[6]

Now you have a year under your belt and you are getting the hang of this college way of life. You are now in your second year of school so you survived freshman year! You may have friends that are no longer in school with you because they probably failed many of their classes, figured out that college wasn't for them, or found another avenue to fulfill their career goals. Whatever the case may be, you must continue to do your very best in your classes. It may be hard to believe that many of your friends will not walk that stage with you because college may not be for them. Being a college graduate, I realize that it is not for everyone.

---

[6] "Wisdom." Def. 1a-2. *Webster's New Notebook Dictionary*. 2000.

Everyone cannot handle the pressure of tough college classes. However, you will go on to succeed in your classes and walk across that stage when your tassel comes calling.

Accordingly, freshman year has allowed you to gain wisdom in passing your classes. Your first year has taught you how to take notes, how to read meticulously, prepare for exams, and use your peers effectively to get through courses. Forming study groups in my classes was a lifesaver. Two or three heads is better than one. Everyone brings something different to the table when studying for a quiz or an exam. I have found that students learn differently. Everyone does not process what the professor lectures in the same manner. Therefore, when studying in groups, different students can bring their own approach to the material that is likely to be covered on exams. My last three years in college, I received straight A's because I learned how to study with other people. My classmates and I would form groups of three to four students to construct a study guide to best cover the information that the professor repeatedly talked about in class.

## Start Thinking about your Major

During your first year, most of you took general classes or elective classes that were prerequisites to most majors. During your sophomore year, you should still take some general classes but it's important that you get a start on taking some classes that will be needed for your particular major. Getting a jump on taking a few major classes will lighten your load as you progress in your educational career. If you are taking five classes a semester, two of those classes should fulfill your major requirements.

## Hypotheticals

*If Tiffany is a second year Biology student, she should take a language, art, and history course as electives; her other two classes should be science related so that she can satisfy her Biology major requirements.*

*If Matthew is a second year History student, he should take a language, music, and political science course as electives; his other two classes should be history related so that he can satisfy his History major requirements.*

REMEMBER: Each major requires a specific number of courses taken in that area. Keep track of your major classes so that you can know where you stand in terms of graduating on time...remember that handy dandy catalog.

## What Should I Major In?

This is a question that every college student will think and/or ask themselves at some point before or during their college career. Unfortunately, there is no clear-cut answer to this question. Instead of asking what should I major in, you should ask yourself what do I enjoy doing? What you enjoy doing is what you would want to make a career out of. You should have passion for your career because if you love it, it will be gratifying and rewarding. Some students may find themselves in a situation where they do not have a clue about what they want to do as an adult and they don't know what they enjoy doing. One way to find out what you enjoy doing is to volunteer with different organizations. In your school's community, there will be organizations that will service the elderly, infants, school age children, the disabled, rescued animals and etc. Working alongside different types of individuals will allow you to find a niche that you can make a career out of.

Not only does volunteering allow you to figure out your career choice, but it also helps you to network with people working in that field. Volunteering will only take a few hours out of your day and will be worked around your schedule. It will be fun and productive because it will lead you to different career choices. The organizers and employers of these organizations will be watching you and witnessing your strong work ethic. This could land you a part-time job and maybe a full-time career once you graduate from college. So remember to be on time, courteous, and at your best because you never know who is watching.

## Hypotheticals

*Matt is unsure of what he wants to do when he graduates from college but he is volunteering down at the local hospital. After hands-on experience with patients and health care professionals, he is seriously thinking about becoming a medical doctor.*

*Lisa does not know what to major in but she likes acting. She volunteers at the film festivals that come to town every summer. She now realizes that she wants to be a movie producer or director. Her hard work at the film festivals was recognized by one of the film directors at the festival who asked her to help with an independent film.*

## Researching Different Fields

Researching different fields is very important. Researching will allow you to learn the ins and outs of a career. This will include what the career will offer such as the outlook, pay, work environment, hours, travel requirements, promotions, and growth within the company. You have to thoroughly research the occupation that you are interested in. This entails discovering the primary duties of that occupation. Don't put yourself in a situation where you ask yourself 'Why did I choose this field?' There should not be any surprises or things that you didn't expect to take place. This does not mean that you are going to know everything when entering a field, but if you prepare yourself, you will be able to adapt to whatever it is you have to do.

## *What's the required level of education for entrance into your field?*

After researching the duties of the occupation, you should consider the required level of education needed for that career. It's important to know if you need technical or vocational training, an associate's degree, a bachelor's degree, graduate school, and/ or any other special certifications. Knowing what type of education is needed in the beginning, will save you lots of sweat and tears later on. Education is time consuming and can be very expensive so don't waste time or money if you don't have to.

### What Not To Do

Jimmy is in his senior year of college and has aspirations of becoming a dental hygienist. Throughout his college career, he has taken numerous science courses but none in dental health. After visiting his academic counselor, he learns that he should have taken Dental Hygiene courses at the community college down the street. It would have only taken two years to earn his degree in Dental Health because it's an associate degree. Now, he has to make a tough decision because he can either start over by enrolling in the college that has the program or he can continue taking classes at his current college and change his career choice. He does not have the money or time to start completely from scratch so Jimmy has decided to continue his science classes in hopes of becoming a scientist or chemist. However, he knows that these particular fields will not be fulfilling.

Tonya has known since her junior year in high school that she wanted to be a child psychologist. She is two months away from graduating from PSU with a BA in Psychology. Within the last few weeks, she has learned that she needs to further her education with a graduate degree in order to become a child psychologist. This was unexpected news because she does not have the money to attend graduate school. In addition, she has not prepared for graduate school nor has she taken any of the entrance exams needed to enroll in one. Does she take the next few months preparing to get accepted in graduate school or does she try to find a job where she can utilize her degree? What if she finds out that she has to have a master's degree (graduate degree) to find any kind of job in her field?

These are tough questions so there aren't easy answers to them. DON'T PUT YOURSELF IN THIS SITUATION. With proper research and preparation, you can avoid this dilemma and choose a career that you want to do.

## *What skills are needed in your field?*

Next, consider the skills needed in order to fulfill your job duties. If you want to be an editor, I can guarantee that you will need to have strong writing and reading comprehension abilities. Likewise, if you have a poor writing ability, then you may find being an editor demanding and complex. You have to find a career that requires the skills that you will excel in. Researching the skills that are needed for that career will help you to match up with that field. If you are a computer wizard and enjoy spending long hours working on them, then you may enjoy being a computer technician of some sort. Why not get paid for doing something you love doing every day?

## *Does your field require you to get certificates and licenses?*

This is related to what education is needed for your field. The type of education you obtain will get you in the door; these additional requirements will *keep* you in the door. It's important to know what these are because they will also be time consuming. It may take anywhere from two weeks to one year to fulfill. A company may or may not pay for this additional education, thus the money may have to come out of your pocket. Knowing this can help you to save money ahead of time instead of taking on an unexpected expense. In addition, knowing this can help you to prepare for the licensure. You can get a start on reading and studying for the particular test in question. Whether it is a written or hands-on exam, you will be prepared for whatever they toss your way. Keep in mind that many companies will not let you continue to work without these credentials, therefore, prepare for them and get them out of the way.

### Do you have room to grow in your field?

This should be a critical factor in your decision to pursue a career. Do you want to be stuck in a career where you will be in the same position for twenty years performing the same mundane roles? If not, research if your career will allow you to grow either laterally or vertically. *Lateral growth* is where you can move to another position and specialize in something different. Lateral growth may come with raises and promotions. *Vertical growth* is where you can move up to a higher position, which will come with higher raises and attractive promotions. No one wants to be at a job where they are stagnant or at a standstill.

Also consider how long it will take you to reach that desired position that you want to obtain. Research the schedule of raises/promotion to see whether you will be where you desire in five or ten years.

## What other occupations can you pursue with the degree you have chosen?

You should prepare for the unexpected. In the event you don't obtain the job that you were seeking, have a plan B and C. When choosing a major, look to see what careers could be embarked upon with that degree. You have to be versatile and able to adapt if things don't go the way you thought they would. In other words, research what other fields you can go into with the degree that you have declared.

### Deeper Look at Me

*When researching a degree in Political Science, I considered all the possible careers that coincided with it. With a Political Science degree I knew that I would be able to go to law school... However, I found out that with this degree I could be a political science teacher, a lobbyist, CIA or FBI agent, social worker, and so on. These fields were also attractive to me because my skill set would allow me to do well in them. I gained a peace of mind in knowing that if I was unable to attend law school there were an ample number of other fields where I could use my degree.*

## Testimonials

"When I graduated college, I embarked upon the business world. I made tons of money but I also worked a ton of hours. During the average week, I worked at least 60 hours. I didn't have time for family or friends. I wish I would have gone into something that I actually enjoyed doing despite the amount of money it entailed."

– Mark

"I am a social worker and some may consider it a low paying job. I must admit, it is. I'm not ashamed to reveal that I make about $31,000 a year. However, I touch many lives on a daily basis. My career allows me to make a difference in the lives of children and their parents. I wouldn't trade my profession for anything in this world."

– Lisa

REMEMBER: Instead of asking what should I major in, you should ask yourself what do I enjoy doing?

TIP: Love what you do and you will enjoy doing what you do.

## Taking a Second Language

*If you don't listen to anything I have written in this book, remember to learn and become fluent in a language different from your own.* Being able to speak another language will make you more marketable in the job force and strengthen your resume. This will help you to become a stand-out and enable employers to pursue you for a position in their company. Currently, heavy competition exists in basically every job market; therefore, get a leg up on other applicants by adding a second language to your repertoire.

**Did You Know?** The six official languages of the United Nations are Arabic, Chinese, English, French, Russian, and Spanish. Visit UN.com for more on these languages and the United Nations.

## Real Life Scenarios

**#1** *Imagine that company X has an opening for a sales position. They received over 100 cover letters and resumes and have narrowed their selection down to two applicants. Both of these applicants have bachelor degrees in the same area. They have similar skill sets and have done an internship. The manager has to pick between two candidates who are basically identical on paper. After reviewing the resumes a bit closer, the manager learns that one of the candidates is fluent in Spanish. This candidate* *would be an asset to the company since it has business relations with other companies in Mexico and Spain. The manager then calls the Spanish speaking applicant in for an interview.*

*#2 Imagine that company Y has an opening for a director of personnel of an Asian services corporation. Two qualified applicants have been called in for an interview. From the interview, the human resources manager learns that both of the candidates can speak Mandarin Chinese. However, when put in a room to interact with Chinese speakers, Cory's speech was more logical and coherent than Bill's speech. Cory later got the position and revealed that he spends at least one hour each night practicing Mandarin. He obtained the position over Bill because of his dedication and consistency in his quest to master another language.*

## Finding the Time to Dedicate to a Second Language

I do admit that your course work will consume a great deal of your time. If you are a full-time student, you will have anywhere from four to eight classes, which may be demanding. These classes may require you to do outside research, multiple papers, and tedious readings. Therefore, you will have to make time to learn another language. Learning another language takes commitment and persistence. It will not be easy but with hard work, you can do it. Here are ten steps to learning a second language...

1.  Pick a language that interests you because it will be easier to grasp if you want to learn it.

2.  Listen to an audio tape/cd (with the language you're studying) for at least fifteen minutes a day.

3.  Open your language text book and spend at least fifteen minutes a day reading and going over what you learned in class.

4.  Create a study group with your classmates so that you all can go over the material learned in class.

5.  Ask your instructor for one on one time so that he/she can help you where there are difficulties.

6.  In your spare time, rent movies that are spoken in the language that you are learning.

7.  Try to buy magazines and newspapers written in the language that you are learning.

8.  Join a club at your college/university specific to the language that you are learning.

9.  Plan to take a study abroad trip in the country that speaks the language that you are learning in order to immerse yourself.

10. **No matter how complicated it may be to learn a second language, NEVER GIVE UP.**

## Deeper Look at Me

*Go to www.collegecanbeasy.com to find out my harsh reality of not learning a second language.*

## Studying Abroad

*What is a study abroad program?*

Even though this question may seem self-explanatory, it's one that is frequently asked. A study abroad program is where students can take classes and receive course credit while studying in another country. It's an excellent opportunity for students to learn outside of the traditional classroom while traveling the world. A study abroad program can be short as two weeks and as long as a whole academic year. Many colleges will categorize study abroad programs by the countries that they will be held in. For example, your college may have four programs offered in Asia, two in Europe, and five in Africa. So keep in mind what area or region of the world you would like to travel to.

During your second semester of your sophomore year, I recommend that you embark on a study abroad to another country. By this time, you should have taken most of your core/prerequisite classes and maybe you are just beginning to take classes needed to fulfill your major. This is an important transition period because you will be going from an underclassman to an upperclassman, in which, the classes will become more demanding. For this reason, I recommend studying abroad at this point in your college career because your schedule may be more lenient and flexible. As a junior and senior, you will have a full plate and it may be difficult to find time for things other than a part-time job, studying, reading lengthy chapters, and writing papers. However, if it isn't possible for you to study abroad during this time, take one during the first semester of your junior year.

**Why Should you Study Abroad?**

Studying abroad can be a gratifying and enlightening experience, especially if you have never left the country before. You will be able to immerse yourself in a culture that's different from your own. You can experience how another group of people live, learn, think, eat, raise their children, and handle their day to day business. Through this process, you will become a well-rounded person because studying abroad will give you self-awareness, culture sensitivity, patience, diversity, and respect for things that are dissimilar.

**TIP:** Studying abroad is also a resume booster for catching the eyes of future employers!!

## So you Want to Study Abroad?

Before applying for a study abroad program, obtain a passport if you do not already have one. The earlier you apply for it, the less stress you will have later because passports can take up to two months to be mailed to you. There may be problems that arise with paperwork or other issues that may take an extended amount of time before you receive it. For this reason, apply for your passport at least four months before the start of the trip. Passports can be obtained at certain Post Offices, libraries, the Department of Motor Vehicles.

When deciding to take a study abroad trip, you should consider where in the world you want to go. Deciding on a country to travel to can be stressful and overwhelming, but deciding the best fit for you will be very rewarding. Here are some tips in deciding where you should take your study abroad trip...

- Pick a country that you have studied and/or researched in the past that way you will be somewhat familiar with their culture.

- If you have taken foreign language courses, pick a country where you can use this language to be able to communicate with the native people. This will help to ease the language barrier and frustration that comes along with not knowing the language that everyone is speaking around you.

- Pick a country where you are familiar with their foods and enjoy eating them. This will ease the transition of experiencing culture shock from being in a new country.

- Pick a country that has the type of weather that you are used to. If you are from Florida and used to warm weather, it may be difficult to get adjusted to the temperatures in Russia during the winter. Weather should be a critical factor in deciding where to travel. It can make the difference between having a great time or a terrifying one.

- Check the currency exchange...since the US dollar is losing value compared to other currencies, you should consider the cost of living in the country you have chosen. When visiting, you want to be able to dine out, do a little shopping, take a trip out on the town, etc. If you are on a budget and travel to a place with a high cost of living, you may find yourself unable to enjoy some of the local tourist attractions.

## How to Study Abroad?

Studying abroad is an intricate process. When deciding to study abroad, you have to look at what classes you must take before graduation. It's important to remember to take study abroad classes that you can use towards your degree. It would be wise to sit down with your academic advisor and ask what courses you should pursue abroad. Once you know what classes you will take abroad, it's imperative that you ask the department head (the person in charge of the department where you are pursuing your major) if those courses will fulfill your degree requirements.

Once you know what classes to take, you can begin to look at different study abroad programs that are offered through your school or even through another institution. Choose a program that will meet your academic needs. The ideal study abroad will be a place that you want to visit and that will allow you to fulfill your academic requirements. Thoroughly researching a study abroad program will ensure that you make all the right decisions in regards to your economic and academic status.

Next, you should contact the program director of the program/programs that you are considering. The program director can give you a synopsis of what the study abroad will be like. You can ask all the questions that you need in order to ease your anxiety about going to a foreign place. Most likely this person has headed the program in the past and has plenty of information about the dos and don'ts of studying in that country. Most program directors will have an information session about the study abroad program where students can learn information and find out what is expected from them and the trip. If the director doesn't show pictures from previous trips, ask if they have any so that you can get a glimpse of that country before you head over. Also, the director may get students who have taken the trip to share their experiences with those interested in taken it. This would be a great opportunity for you to get a student's point of view about studying abroad.

After researching different programs and meeting with people who will head them, you should check and see if your institution offers a seminar for students who would like to study abroad; this will allow you to interact with professors and other students who have gone abroad. Most likely, it will be a general preview of what students should expect before, during, and after going abroad. The globe trekking session will probably be held in the Study Abroad Office. Many colleges and universities have this office available to students to advise them before they go abroad. In fact, this office will have different brochures and pamphlets on different programs that will be offered abroad. You can also inquire about scholarships and other funding through this office. If your institution is similar to mine, the study abroad office will give a minimal scholarship to students who want to go abroad. Usually the requirements are: the student must possess a certain grade point average, complete an application, write an essay on why they want to study abroad, and submit one or two reference letters. They may require more or less depending on the rules and regulations set up by that office.

REMEMBER: Scholarships given by the study abroad office will have deadlines that you must adhere to in order to obtain funding. Also, in exchange for the scholarship you receive, the office may ask you to spend a certain amount of hours sharing your experiences with students who also want to go abroad. This would be a great way for you to give back to students who are following in your footsteps.

## Funding your study abroad $$$$$

It's important to note that the study abroad program and the tuition paid to your institution are separate costs. The program has costs associated with attending that study abroad, and you will have to pay your college or university tuition in order to take courses and receive credit.

Before you start thinking about funding your trip, it would be wise to pick a program that you can afford and one where airfare and hotel costs are included in the trip price. You will find that some programs will include your round trip airfare and hotel costs and others will not. If you choose one that will include your airfare and hotel costs, this will save you time because you will not have to search for plane tickets or book hotel rooms. It also will be more expensive if you are not paying the group rates that many program directors take advantage of especially when a large number of students are traveling.

**TIP:** If you get refund checks from your financial aid...SAVE THEM! After you have fulfilled all of your financial obligations, put the remainder of the money in a savings account. This money can be used to study abroad!

In case you are unaware of the cost of studying abroad, **it can be expensive**. When traveling to another country, flights and hotel costs can reach high amounts. As mentioned above, you may receive a scholarship through your institution's study abroad office **but** it will not begin to cover all of your expenses while traveling overseas. However, with preparation and a strategy, you can get enough scholarships and other funding that will send you abroad. Hence, you should try to receive as many scholarships as possible.

Here are the keys to obtaining scholarships to fund your study abroad...

- Research many different avenues to receive funding. This means checking with different corporations and organizations to see if they have money set aside to assist students with their education. Check with Chick-fil-A, Kroger, Publix, Wal-Mart, Target, Taco Bell, Best Buy, AT&T, and Verizon, just to name a few.

- Check with your church or the community church to see if they can help you fundraise for your trip abroad. They should be happy to help a college student travel to another country and experience a different way of life.

- Ask family members for their help. If 20 people in your family gave you $100 each, you would have $2,000 that would go towards your study abroad.

- Search the internet for different study abroad scholarships. Millions of dollars are wasted each year because many students do not take advantage of scholarships that can be found online.

- Check to see if your study abroad program offers scholarships. Your program director may give out one or two scholarships on a competitive basis. Make sure to apply for these scholarships in a timely manner.

- Be prepared to write convincing essays to obtain a scholarship. You will have to convey your thoughts and feelings and explain why you should get money from that person, company, corporation, or organization.

REMEMBER: There may be hundreds of students applying for the same scholarship that you are—so what's going to set you apart from them?

- Start searching for scholarships at least four months before you are set to leave.

- Be cordial and gracious.

- Stay humble.

- Stay persistent and don't give up on the search for free money.

**Your Last Option...**

If you are unsuccessful at finding and receiving scholarships, I suggest you take out a loan to finance your trip. This should be your last option because I know that there is lots of free money floating around out there. Don't be reluctant to take out a loan because your trip will be well worth the money that you borrow. Even though you have to pay it back, you will have long lasting memories that will be irreplaceable.

What the US Senate has to say about studying abroad...

In Senate Resolution 308, 2006 was designated the **'year of study abroad'** to encourage students to travel and study in a foreign country[7]. The resolution states 13 reasons why students should do so:

1. Ensuring that the citizens of the United States are globally literate is the responsibility of the educational system of the United States.

2. Educating students internationally is an important way to share the values of the United States, to create goodwill for the United States around the world, to work toward a peaceful global society, and to increase international trade.

3. 79 percent of people in the United States agree that students should have a study abroad experience sometime during college, but only 1

---

[7] *Vistawide.* World Languages & Cultures. <http://www.vistawide.com/studyabroad/year_of_study_abroad2006.htm>

percent of students from the United States currently study abroad each year.

4.   Study abroad programs help people from the United States to be more informed about the world and to develop the cultural awareness necessary to avoid offending individuals from other countries.

5.   87 percent of students in the United States between the ages of eighteen and twenty-four cannot locate Iraq on a map, 83 percent cannot find Afghanistan, 58 percent cannot find Japan, and 11 percent cannot even find the United States.

6.   Studying abroad exposes students from the United States to valuable global knowledge and cultural understanding and forms an integral part of their education.

7.   The security, stability, and economic vitality of the United States are suffering from a shortage of professionals with international knowledge and foreign language skills.

8.   Federal agencies, educational institutions, and corporations in the United States are suffering from a shortage of professionals with international knowledge and foreign language skills.

9.   Institutions of higher education in the United States are struggling to graduate enough students with the language skills and cultural competence necessary to meet the current demands

of business, government, and educational institutions.

10. Studying abroad influences subsequent educational experiences, decisions to expand or change academic majors, and decisions to attend graduate school.

11. Some of the core values and skills of higher education are enhanced by participation in study abroad programs.

12. Study abroad programs not only open doors to foreign language learning, but also empower students to better understand themselves and others through a comparison of cultural values and ways of life.

13. Study abroad programs for students from the United States can provide specialized training and practical experiences not available at institutions in the United States.

## Deeper Look at Me
### Study Abroad

*I wasn't the traditional college student, and I was not enjoying campus life. I didn't live on campus so my college experience was suffering. One day as I was eating lunch, I began to think about traveling to another country to study at another university. I knew this would be a great way to add excitement to my college life while experiencing another culture.*

Thus, my first step was visiting my university's study abroad office. It was there where I was able to learn about the different programs offered. It was also there where I found the program that I attended. It was called '2008 Summer Study in China Program' and the dates were from June 8 to July 10. After looking at my academic transcript, I learned that I could take one elective and one major class while studying in China. I registered for a World Geography and a Criminal Justice course. After getting approval from the head of the political science department, my classes were in place for the trip.

Next, I had a face-to-face meeting with one of the professors that was going on the trip. He gave me tips on traveling abroad as well as the dos and don'ts about staying in China. He also informed me that the program offered two scholarships. Fortunately, I applied for a scholarship and won it! That scholarship money put me $500 dollars closer to having enough money to pay for my trip. I also applied for the IEF (International Education Fund) scholarship through the study abroad office at my school. A career counselor told me about another scholarship given by the Women's Expo and I applied for it. I wrote an essay on why I should receive the scholarship and sent them my academic transcript. A month later, I was invited to their conference where they would announce the scholarship recipient. To my surprise, I was announced as the winner, so I had to give an acceptance speech in front of a small amount of people. But, those three scholarships were still not enough money to cover all of my expenses.

Hence, I had to find another strategy to search for more money. I begin to ask local companies, family, and church members for contributions. It was then when I raised enough money to pay for my trip and have spending money while I was abroad. **I made sure to buy small presents as a token of my appreciation for the individuals who helped me.** If I could go from $0 to $4,000 in two months to study abroad, then YOU can do the same thing or even better!!!!

Studying abroad was the highlight of my college years. From eating Chinese food with the locals to shopping down bizarre back alleys, I experienced something never before imagined. From climbing the Great Wall of China, to seeing the Terracotta Warriors and the actual location where they were discovered, my imagination became reality. From walking through the Forbidden City and Tiananmen Square, I became a part of Chinese history.

REMEMBER: If you do not currently have enough money to study in another country, don't let that discourage you because someone will help you raise the money to go!

The big secret in life is there is no secret. Whatever your goal, you can get there if you're willing to work.

– Oprah Winfrey

# CHAPTER | 3

# YOU ARE OFFICIALLY AN UPPERCLASSMAN...WELCOME TO YOUR JUNIOR YEAR

You have two down and two more to go so keep your eyes on the prize. From my experience, junior year is a peculiar year. Once you are here, you may start getting comfortable and relaxed as if you are finished.

REMEMBER: You are only halfway there.

You are so close yet so far away because this is a momentous year. This is the year that will determine your future beyond college. This should be a year filled with hard work and preparation.

Let's make sure that you are on the right track...

**Have you declared a major yet?**

I hope that you have been thinking about what major you are going to declare. The clock is ticking and you should declare a major soon. This will give you time to change it later if you decide to major in something else. Two factors to always consider are TIME and MONEY because they can make or break your college career. You don't want to waste time in school because you are unsure of what to study. Likewise, you don't want to spend unnecessary money on classes that you don't need.

If you're still unsure of what to major in, keep volunteering with different organizations to find out what your interests are. Later, I will discuss the possibility of an internship for you to gain experience and to find out if you enjoy a particular field. Don't feel pressured to pick a major for the sake of picking one. Make sure that it is what you want to pursue. As I discussed in the sophomore chapter, you want to pick a major that you have researched. Let me reiterate that it would be wise for you to ask your academic advisor and professors about the majors you're considering. Make it your business to know what type of jobs you can obtain with the major/majors that you choose.

REMEMBER: If you have not decided a major before junior year, pick one before the start of the second semester (of your junior year).

Once you pick a major, here come major classes...

## Major Classes

Major classes are those that are required by a particular major. These classes prepare you for your specific area of study. As a junior, your schedule should include two or three of these types of classes. You don't want to wait until your senior year and overload your schedule with these classes only because they will require intensive work. If you are unsure of what your major classes are, ASK YOUR ACADEMIC ADVISOR. You want to make sure that you are on track for graduation. YOU WILL NOT GRADUATE IF YOU DO NOT SATISFY/COMPLETE all areas specified by your major requirements. I apologize if my words are coming across as repetitive or redundant but it is very important that you know what classes to take and when to complete them.

Make sure to check your academic transcript as you progress in your classes. **CHECK WITH YOUR ACADEMIC ADVISOR TO OBTAIN YOUR TRANSCRIPT.**

## Internships

An internship is where you will work for a company or organization usually without pay in exchange for work experience. Every now and again, you might come across an internship that will offer monetary benefits. However, money should not be a factor in your decision to take on an internship.

Networking, experience, and the opportunity to receive course credit should be factors in your decision.

## Networking

When you intern at a company, business, organization, etc. you will be surrounded by people who are doing exactly what you are striving to do. They are where you hope to be in two to four years so use this time to learn everything that they are willing to teach. Ask these professionals questions about the field they are working in and why they chose it. Ask them for pointers and advice about entering that field. Most likely, they will let you shadow them to watch their daily activities. This will allow you to get a glimpse of what a day in the life looks like for individuals working in a certain career. This is where you will determine if the career is a perfect fit for you or if it is something that you no longer want to pursue. The latter situation will allow you time to change your mind and search other career options. You can only win with doing an internship because it gives you an opportunity to test the waters and see what you will or will not enjoy doing as a career. You also have a great chance of getting hired by the person over your internship especially if you demonstrate hard work and professionalism.

On the contrary, if you do not take an internship, you may major in something that conflicts with your personality. After going through years of schooling, you may find that you dislike your field and wish you had chosen another one. Let's eliminate the "would of, should of, or could of," and take an internship to be sure we will be doing something that we love getting out of bed for.

Besides, you never know who you will meet while doing an internship. You could be working beside a human resources manager that will hire you straight out of college, a CEO of an upstart company, vice president of a marketing firm, or a stockbroker looking for young students to train as Wall Street brokers.

REMEMBER: Your internship is your way in the door once you close out your college career. So work hard even when you think no one is looking.

**Experience**

Not only will an internship allow you to network, but it will also give you valuable work experience in the field that you are pursuing. Most employers will employ a person with experience and no college degree over someone with a college degree and no work experience. Experience means that a person will not require much on the job training, which will save a company money and time. You also will be able to transition into a job a lot smoother if you've gained previous knowledge and experience. Your learning curve will be a lot more narrow if you already possess skills and familiarity with a particular career.

**Real Life Scenarios**

*Brett is applying for a public relations position after recently graduating from college. He never completed an internship while in school because his major did not require it. His advisor and parents suggested that he complete one, but he opted not to. Although he has a Communication's degree, he is having trouble landing a job at a public relations firm. After interviewing with a potential employer, he learned that his lack of experience in public relations was impeding on his ability to obtain employment. He then had to find an unpaid internship with a PR firm and hope that it would develop into a career. Instead of finding a full time career, Brett has to search for an internship to gain work experience.*

**To avoid being in this situation, listen to me and do an internship while in school.**

> REMEMBER: Gaining experience through an
> internship will be beneficial for you and your
> future employer.

## Opportunity to Receive Course Credit

After networking and obtaining valuable experience and training, your internship can allow you to get credit towards your course/courses. This will allow you to complete classes outside of being in a physical classroom or lecture hall. Colleges and universities give students the opportunity to complete classes through internships because they understand the importance of students getting out in the field to receive hands on experience. What student doesn't want to receive course credit without having to do rigorous readings, lengthy research papers, quizzes, and exams?

Once you get approval from the department head or internship program coordinator for taking the internship, you should ask him/her what all the requirements are for receiving course credit and how much course credit you can receive. Knowing the requirements will allow you to work on them ahead of time while the information is fresh in your memory. For example, if the department head requires a fifty page diary of your experience, you will be able to work on it daily instead of waiting to after you complete your internship to have another big responsibility before you.

REMEMBER: Internships at larger companies, businesses, and organizations usually will have you complete minuscule daily activities such as filing, data entry, running errands, and small janitorial duties. This is due to the fact that they have many employees who perform different duties. On the other hand, interning at smaller companies, businesses, and organizations usually will allow you to perform administrative and hands-on duties such as writing memos, attending meetings, updating their website, and organizing financial records.

For this reason, I recommend interning at a smaller organization or business to really understand the nature of what they do.

You should be able to ask your academic advisor and professors about where to find internships. If your college/university has a career services department, someone there will probably be able to help you go about getting one.

**Get a Mentor**

I recommend you to get a mentor that will help you with your career decisions. Mentors can be anybody from one of your professors, previous teachers, to a pastor, owner of a local business in your community, etc. Preferably, a mentor should be a person who is in the field that you want to pursue. They will serve as your personal advisor and you can ask them any questions that you may have about that field.

Mentors are important because they have life experience that will help you along. You can learn from their successes and failures. You actually gain an advantage from learning from someone's mistakes by bypassing the trial and error period while climbing up the ladder of success.

I've learned that people love sharing knowledge and the secrets to their success. Most successful people want to have someone that they can take under their wings and help them blossom. You should always surround yourself with successful people because you will begin to think and act as they do.

## Stay Focused and Build on your First Two Years

- You are still in school so continue to do what got you here.

- Continue to study hard and put your best foot forward.

- If your grade point average (GPA) is not where you want it to be, continue to work hard to raise it. Strive to graduate with at least a 3.5 GPA (*Cum Laude*). That will stand out on your resume, and on grad & law school applications.

- Continue to read your text books so that you can retain the information learned in class.

- Continue to build amicable relationships with your professors. Next year, you are going to need recommendations from them. From time to time, stay after class and talk one on one with your professors so that they know who you are.

- Stand out in class by answering and asking questions.

- Continue to form study groups and positive relations with your peers. You will be surprised to find out how students can help each other.

- Keep and file some of your outstanding research papers that you recently wrote. **You may have to submit them as writing samples to get a job or internship.**

- If you have not already done so, start developing your resume. Visit your college's career center for help with your resume.

- Continue learning a foreign language.

- Start thinking about if you are going to continue your education. This may entail visiting another college, researching other programs, filling out paperwork, preparing for tests such as the LSAT, GRE, MCAT, GMAT, etc.

- Only if it is possible, try and take another study abroad trip.

REMEMBER: Always keep your research/term papers. Many employers will ask for a writing sample to evaluate your penmanship.

"A good exercise for the heart is to bend down and help another up"

– Anonymous

## Are you Involved on Campus?

I don't want to over emphasize the importance of being a social college student, but you will obtain an enriching college experience by being involved on campus. Being involved isn't just going to parties and drinking excessively. Contrary to many beliefs, being social is joining different clubs and organizations. In these organizations, you will meet people that you will develop lifelong friendships and lasting memories with.

You probably won't remember getting drunk and passing out, but you will remember volunteering in the community, participating in different rallies, putting on different events, and listening to prominent speakers that come to campus to speak. Make sure that your college career is well rounded and fulfilling. Once you graduate, work is thrown to the forefront so there is less time for trying to relive the fun that you should have enjoyed while in school.

Most colleges and universities will have an office for student life and leadership. This office will be a place for students to go and find out about different organizations on campus. Make this office a place that you visit frequently in order to get acquainted with your peers and campus activities!

## Go ΓΡΕΕΚ (GREEK)

**Research Says...**

*Statistical research indicates that membership in a Greek organization is positively related to cognitive development, which is a result of their social involvement (Pike).*

*A study of 600 freshmen and 1,000 seniors at the University of Missouri revealed that Greek freshmen reported making substantially greater gains in interpersonal skills development than did independent freshmen (Pike).*

*Greek seniors reported greater gains in general education, intellectual development, and interpersonal skills (Pike).*

*Greek affiliation is not negatively related to academic involvement (Pike). Research found that this is due to the fact that fraternities and sororities stress the importance of academic success (Pike).*

*For African American students at both Historically Black Colleges & Universities (HBCUs) and Public White Institutions (PWIs), Greeks had a significantly higher grade point average than non-Greek's (Kimbrough and Hutcheson).*

*Black Greek Organization membership enhance student involvement and leadership development for African Americans for college and beyond (Kimbrough and Hutcheson).*

Hence, joining a Greek letter organization can be a gratifying experience that will bring you many lasting memories. The sisterhood or brotherhood that you join will last a lifetime.

## Why should you join a Greek letter organization?

- It will teach you discipline and loyalty that you have never experienced before.
- It cultivates leadership, perseverance, willpower, and esteem.
- It is a life-changing event that will be academically and personally enhancing.
- If anyone in your family has joined the same organization, you will be carrying on a legacy.

## When should I pledge/join a Greek letter organization?

I recommend that you pledge a Greek letter organization the first semester of your junior year. By this time, you should have established a solid college career and obtained a good GPA.

Most colleges will require you to complete a certain amount of classes and obtain a certain GPA before you are able to pledge.

REMEMBER: Timing is very important when you decide to pledge any Greek organization. You will have to balance your studies, personal life, and work with pledging.

## How should I join a Greek letter organization?

You should research the organization that you want to become a member of. Make sure that you are familiar with their history and ideals.

Contact the president or vice president of the organization to find out how to join.

If your college has an office of student life and leadership, visit and ask how to join that organization.

Be persistent and keep track of events that the organization holds so that you can attend some of them.

Greek life is very **sacred** so watch what you say and the manner in which you say it to leaders of the organization.

REMEMBER: *When speaking about Greek Organizations, "less is best."*

**What not to do...**

- Join an organization if you're not dedicated and committed to their goals. If you do this, you will become a tee-shirt wearer (a person who joins an organization and does not put any work into it).

- Join an organization without researching its history and impact on campus.

- Join an organization only because your friends are doing it. Make sure it's something that you really want to do.

- Join an organization without taking pride in it. Your organization will be what you make it.

- Pledge a Greek organization with a struggling GPA.

- Pledge a Greek organization only to gain popularity and accolades.

**TIP**: Make sure that you give 110 percent to any organization that you join. You will get out whatever you put in.

## Deeper Look at Me

*Before I joined a sorority, my college experience was empty. I didn't have any meaningful relationships with my peers and I was longing for sisterhood.*

*After joining, my college and personal life benefited tremendously. I joined a sisterhood where my sisters stood up for each other. We volunteered in the community, went shopping, dined out, had sleepovers, and enjoyed each other as sisters. It feels good knowing that we belong to an organization rich in tradition and purpose.*

*I love them, and I'm glad that I joined a sorority. If you join a Greek organization, I hope that you have a pleasant experience also.*

# CHAPTER | 4
## YOU MADE IT...SENIOR YEAR

*Don't Get Senioritis.*

–L.M. Bedell

This is the year that you have been waiting for since you graduated from high school. I remember walking across the stage in high school and thinking "in four years I will be walking across another grand stage."

Let me be the first to tell you that your senior year is a triumphant year. You have made it through the previous levels of schooling to get to the verge of graduating from a higher learning institution. Whether you are attending a technical school, arts or culinary arts school, institute, junior college, or university; you should be proud that you've made it thus far. However, do not get into relaxation mode until you walk across that stage and receive your diploma/degree.

You have come too far to lose track on the trail that you have worked extremely hard to pave. Senior year is a particularly delicate period in your college career. At this point, you are inching towards the next step in your life. I'm going to help you make the best out of it so that your transition into the "real world" will be less stressful and overwhelming.

## Another Internship

Even though you probably took an internship during your junior year, I recommend that you take another one during the **first semester of your senior year**. Thus, it should be in a different field than the previous internship you completed.

This would be extremely beneficial if you have two or more career choices in mind. You will be able to take internships in fields that you want to pursue. You will also find out if you like/dislike aspects of these particular careers. I do not want you to graduate from college and not know what to expect in the field that you have chosen.

The number of internships that you take is completely up to you. I understand that work, academics, and social activities can be overwhelming. However, they will only help you in the long run as a resume booster and as a way to gain hands on experience.

## Real Life Scenarios

*Bailey, who is only three months away from graduation, is still unsure of what career she wants to pursue once she finishes college. Marketing and insurance risk management are two fields on the top of her list. As a junior, she interned at a sports marketing firm where she learned a lot about sports and tactful advertising. She enjoyed this internship and found a new love for sports.*

*Last semester, she interned with an insurance adjuster. She didn't really enjoy the work and eventually gave up the internship. From her two internships, she has focused on sports marketing. She put in an application for two professional sports teams in her city and is waiting to hear back from their human resources department.*

## What are the benefits of taking multiple internships as in the case of Bailey?

- It saves time. Instead of wasting time after graduation trying to figure out what you want to do, you can focus on what you **know** you want to do.

- It cuts down on frustration. Instead of landing a job where you are going to be unhappy and not fulfilled, you can get the job that makes you want to get out of bed early.

- It helps you to figure out where your passion is. Once you know where your passion lies, you can channel that energy into your job search that will make you stand out to employers.

REMEMBER: Your situation may be totally opposite of Bailey's, but you can learn from her experience. If possible, taking multiple internships will not hinder but HELP YOU.

## Career Building

You probably will hear this word throughout your college career. Don't just let this word go in one ear and out the other.

Career building is getting involved in areas of your field of interest pertaining to the job you want to pursue.

## HOW DO I SUCCESSFULLY CAREER BUILD?

*Networking*: Networking will connect you with people that are in the position that you want to be in. Volunteering, internships, campus and community events, charity events, fundraisers, etc. are great networking venues that will link you with important people.

*Career Counseling*: If possible, visiting your college's career center to receive professional advice is equally important to networking. In fact, it is a form of networking because career counselors may have friends that could possibly hire you. They understand the job market and can give you pointers on the field that you are pursuing.

*Resume and Cover letter:* The presentation of your resume is your introduction to future employers, graduate and law schools. We live in a competitive world where there are lots of qualified individuals competing for the same jobs. So what's going to set you apart from everyone else? That's why your resume **must** be professional and make a statement.

Things to remember when creating or updating your resume...

1.  Make sure your name is **BOLD** and is at least in size 16 font.

2.  If you have graduated college, put your college education information, but do not include your high school information. People will know that you have graduated high school or received a GED if you attended college.

3.  Make sure that your education, work and volunteer experience (in this order) takes up the bulk of your resume. This information will be the focus of your resume. This outlines how your training can be used on the perspective job.

4.  Make sure that your resume is in chronological order with your most recent activity first.

5.   Do not have special or unusual theme fonts. Try to stick with Times New Roman or Calibri. You want to put more emphasis on your training and skills, not the lettering.

6.   Use one color, black, throughout your resume. It should be only one dominant color.

7.   Do not put pictures of yourself or of anything else on your resume. By not putting a picture of yourself on there, you lessen the chances of being profiled by the way you look.

8.   Your resume should not be longer than **ONE PAGE.** Unless you have more than ten years of experience and multiple degrees, stick to the one page rule.

9.   Make sure that your objective is a clear, defined sentence of what you want to achieve in one line. Here are actual objectives from three of my resumes...

- **Objective:** Seeking an AmeriCorps position with Hands on Atlanta.

- **Objective:** Seeking an exciting and innovative internship with Radiculture Records.

- **Objective:** Seeking the Personal Assistant position with Madison Financial Group.

10.   Be sure to use spell check to ensure correct spelling and grammar; never use slang or inappropriate words.

11. When putting an email on your resume, make sure it's *professional*. It should contain your name and/or numbers. Nicknames or stage names are inappropriate and takes away the effectiveness of your resume. Examples include:

    sweetbaby1234@gmail.com,
    sexygirl22@student.pu.edu,
    hotrodLarry@yahoo.com ☹

    Do you think an employer would take you seriously with an email similar to these?

12. You don't want your email to represent a negative image of you.

Here are some sample resumes and a cover letter:

## MARTHA A. BRIAN

889 Cub Hill Road
City, State, Zip Code
(xxx) xxx-xxxx
E-mail:brian@xxxxx.com

**CAREER OBJECTIVE**  A position in an elementary school utilizing my academic
knowledge and practical experience

**EDUCATION**  Bachelor of Science, Early Childhood Education, May 2002
State University, City, State
Certified preschool to third grade, State
Completed NTE, July 2002

**STUDENT TEACHING**
April-May 2002  **St. Thomas More School, City, State**
Planned lessons for kindergarten students.
Managed classroom: organized students and their activities.

March 2002  **Pot Springs Elementary School, City, State**
Under supervision, planned and taught lessons for second graders.
Assisted in creating positive learning atmosphere.

**RELATED EXPERIENCE**
Spring 2001  **Pleasant Plains Elementary School, City, State**
*Musical Director:* Selected music, rehearsed and
accompanied 20 elementary and junior high students in a
musical review and variety show for P.T.A.

Summer 2000  **Northeast YMCA, City, State**
*Camp Counselor:* Taught first and second grade
disadvantaged students math, reading, and language.
Helped children develop skills in math and reading.

Spring 2000  **St. Dominic School, City, State**
*Teacher aide, volunteer:* Taught first and second grade math,
reading and language. Helped children develop skills in all areas

**INTERESTS**  Music, reading, travel

Figure 20: Sample Chronological Resume - 1

**BRIAN P. SULLIVAN**
110 Morningside Drive
City, State, Zip Code
(xxx) xxx-xxxx
sullivan@xxxxx.com

### OBJECTIVE

Management trainee position in banking using organizational and
management skills and leadership ability.

### EDUCATION

State University, City, State
Bachelor of Science, Business Administration
Concentration in Management, May 2002

### MANAGEMENT SKILLS

- Previewed and purchased merchandise
- Gained product knowledge; developed customer service skills and
  improved sales technique
- Supervised inventory control, monetary transactions, and special projects

### ORGANIZATIONAL SKILLS

- Organized procedures for purchasing, credit approvals, and invoicing
- Worked with buyers in showroom, planning and implementing fashion shows
- Purchased and organized all trimmings for garment production

### LEADERSHIP ABILITIES

- Conducted monthly meetings for retail staff of six
- Planned and supervised fashion shows and photo sessions
- Supervised thirty Boy Scouts; assumed responsibility during change of
  supervisory personnel

### EXPERIENCE

*Assistant Manager*, Boy's Wear, Morgan's Department Store, City, State, (dates)
*Aide to President*, Amy Marsh, Inc. City, State, (dates)
*Management Trainee*, R & M Enterprises, City, State, (dates)
*Trim Buyer*, Charles Stewart Company, City, State, (dates)

### REFERENCES UPON REQUEST

Figure 22: Sample Functional Resume - 1

Your present address
City, State, Zip Code
Date

Hiring Person
Title
Organization
Business Address
City, State, Zip Code

Dear _____ :

OPENING PARAGRAPH
- Explain the reason for the letter and/or identify the position you are seeking.
- Mention how you learned of the position (newspaper, Career Placement Center, name of contact).

MIDDLE PARAGRAPH
- Demonstrate knowledge and interest in the organization.
- Address your ability to contribute to the employer's needs.
- Give examples of your relevant qualifications, accomplishments, and skills.
- Refer the reader to the resume for details (can be included in any paragraph if placement is logical).

CLOSING PARAGRAPH
- End with an action statement - a request for a personal interview.
- If you are inquiring about possible employment (not advertised), take the initiative.
- Mention that you will call to arrange an interview at the employer's convenience.
- Express your thanks.

Sincerely yours,

(Handwritten signature)

Your full name, typed

Figure 26: Guidelines for Cover Letters

Images from *Take Hold of Your Future* used with permission from Kuder, Inc. and Dr. JoAnn Harris-Bowlsbey

## VISIT YOUR COLLEGE'S CAREER CENTER FOR RESUME AND COVERLETTER HELP. THEY GET PAID TO HELP YOU...USE THEIR RESOURCES.

## YOU ARE ALMOST THERE

*Triumph often is nearest when defeat seems inescapable.*

– B.C. Forbes

**Thinking About Life Beyond College**

After you have completed your internship(s) and as your classes begin to dwindle, you should start thinking about what the next step is for you. Are you going to take a break, go to graduate or law school, or go into the career world?

If you are going to continue your education, you will need to prepare for the Graduate Record Exam (GRE), Medical College Admission Test (MCAT), or Law School Admissions Test (LSAT), just to name a few. These tests will require diligent studying and preparation. Your college may offer prep courses for these tests that may cost little to nothing. There are several books and manuals that teach you how to take these tests and offer practice exams to show your progress.

> **TIP**: Kaplan has great books and classes that
> will prepare you for graduate
> level schooling.

### Letters of Recommendation

All graduate programs and certain jobs you apply for will request at least two letters of recommendation. You will need to obtain letters of recommendation from your professors, advisors, counselors, or from whoever knows your academic and professional strengths and weaknesses.

What they might need from you in order to write your recommendation:

1.  Unofficial transcript

2.  Resume

3.  Personal Statement, (which is an essay of why you should be accepted into that school).

### If you Decide to Take a Break

If you decide to take a break after graduation, make sure you use your time wisely. This is the time to sharpen your skills and get experience. Here are a couple things to consider when taking a break between college and graduate school:

- If you have not become fluent in another language, do so.

- Consider taking another internship.

- Generate lots of volunteer experience. This will look great on your resume and on grad, med, and law school applications.

- Gain some professional work experience.

- Continue positive relationships with your professors so that they can remember your attributes when writing your letter of recommendations.

- Begin to prepare and take graduate requisite exams.

- Do not take too long of a break. One year is ideal, and two years is the maximum. If you are going back to school, try to reach that goal within two years.

- If you can, travel and enjoy what the world has to offer.

- Enjoy your time off and do some of the things that you weren't able to do while in undergraduate school.

## Deeper Look at Me

*I took time off after graduating to write this book. I hope you have learned a lot thus far. Keep reading, there is more to come!*

*Your expression is the most important thing you can wear.*

– Sid Ascher

### What Are you Posting on Facebook?

Potential employers may check the Facebook and/or Twitter accounts of potential candidates for a position. Thus, if your profile is not set as private, they can see your wall posts, pictures, and updates. You probably won't be reported to Mark Zuckerberg (the founder of Facebook) but be careful of what you are putting on Facebook. If there are obscene pictures and/or vulgar language on your page, an employer may no longer be interested in you as a job candidate.

REMEMBER: An employer or director of an internship program may pose as a student and try to add you as a friend on Facebook. They also might know one of your friends on Facebook. You never know so be mindful and keep your Facebook CLEAN; besides your parents may be your friends on there and I know you will watch what you post if they are looking.

## Go and Get that Job

After getting your resume and cover letter approved by a career counselor, you should start sending it around to different employers that you are interested in. Check to see if your learning institution has a career website where employers post open positions. Usually, they (employers) will give preference to those resumes over any others they receive.

Don't just send your resume to a couple of employers and expect to land a job. It's going to take patience, dedication, and resilience. Don't get discouraged when no one has called you back for an interview. When this happens, this is your cue to work harder and create novel ways to go about your job search. Go after what you want because nothing is going to be handed to you.

## Show your Determination

Throughout your job search, you want to show employers that you **really** want the position. How does one show that he/she really wants the position?

1. Instead of emailing or posting your resume on a career website, find the address of the employer and drop it off at the office to show your face.

2. If you email your resume, indicate in the email that you are extremely interested in the position and that you will give 110 percent to the completion of your job duties.

3. At the close of your email, put a quote at the bottom that relates to the position. For example, I have sent out legal resumes and put "An injustice anywhere is a threat to justice everywhere" at the foot of the email. This is icing on the cake that will give you an edge in getting an interview.

4. After posting or sending your resume via email, wait a week to call and check the status of your application. On the phone, make sure you are cordial and sound eager.

5. After dropping your application off in the office, wait two weeks to call and check the status of your application. On the phone, make sure you are cordial and sound eager.

**They finally called you in for an interview...**

Please understand that just because you got called in for an interview, that doesn't mean that you have the job. You have one foot in the door; now let me give you a few pointers so that you can get that other one in there.

The night before the interview...

- If you are driving to the interview, calculate the distance and time it will take you to get to the interview.

- If possible, drive to the site of the interview just to see how long it will take you to get there. Doing it this way will allow you to give yourself extra time when considering traffic.

- If you haven't done so already, research the company with whom you are interviewing. Know when it was started and by whom. Try to answer who, what, when, where, and why for that company or organization.

TIP: If the company has a mission statement, learn it and commit it to memory. Even mention it during the interview.

- Write down a list of questions that you would like to ask the person who will be interviewing you. This will allow you to learn about the company's operations and the activities of the position in question.

REMEMBER: Asking questions during an interview will show your interest in the company and position.

- Prepare yourself by going over what the employer is searching for in an employee. This means analyzing the job description and thinking about what **you** can offer that company.

**Universal DOs**

- Arrive at least ten minutes earlier than asked of you.

- Dress in business professional attire.

**A. For women** this includes: Wearing a **suit** (blue, black, grey, or brown). Wear an appropriate length **skirt**, avoiding tight skirts and miniskirts. **Blouses** should be cotton or silk in a neutral color. Avoid sleeveless blouses even with a jacket because they are unprofessional. If you wear a **scarf**, make sure it's simple and matches your outfit in color and pattern; a 34-inch square silk scarf is preferred. **Shoes/pumps** should have a 1 ½ inch heel and complement your suit. Avoid open toe shoes, high boots, stiletto heels, and white shoes. Earrings and excessive jewelry should be left at home ("Proper Business Attire and Etiquette").

**B. For men** this includes: Wearing a **suit** (blue, black, grey, or brown) with a dress shirt and suit jacket. Wear a white, off-white, pale, or blue cotton **shirt**. Wear a **silk tie** without loud colors, patterns, images, or designer logos. Wear long black, dark gray, dark brown, or dark blue **socks**. Your **shoes** should be polished and shined. Don't wear heavy cologne[8].

- If you are a male, make sure your hair is cut and/or is neat. Facial hair should also be neat and kept to a minimum.

- If you are a female, make sure your hair is combed and fixed properly.

- Have at least three copies of your resume and cover letter.

- Always be polite and cordial by smiling and saying "yes sir," "yes ma'am."

- During the interview, take notes on what the interviewer is saying. This shows interest and initiative.

- Make eye contact with your interviewer and give firm (yet gentle) handshakes.

---

[8] *Proper Business Attire and Etiquette: Presenting the Complete Package. TCB Solutions*.http://tcbsolutions.net/Proper_Attire_and_etiquette _for_men_and_women.pdf

**TIP:** When shaking someone's hand who is wearing a ring, be especially careful when giving firm handshakes because it could cause discomfort.

- When the interview has concluded, be sure to thank the interviewer for taking the time to interview you.

**Universal Don'ts**

- Do not arrive late.

- Do not over-answer any questions. Answer what they ask you, not what you think they are asking you.

- Do not talk about politics or religion unless they ask you a specific question pertaining to it.

- Do not discuss money unless they ask you what your pay expectations are. If they ask, say that your salary is negotiable.

- Do not chew gum.

- Do not have your cell phone on where it could ring and distract the interviewer. If you must have it with you, make sure it's turned to silent.

- Do not use slang or inappropriate language.

- Do not ask if the interview is over; let them cue you when they are finished.

- Do not leave there without thanking the interviewer for their time.

If they are impressed with you after the interview, they will tell you that they will call you back in for a second interview. Sometimes it may be a couple days to a few weeks before they finally get back with you so expect to play the waiting game. Therefore, here are a couple rules while playing the waiting game:

Rule 1- Wait about one week after the interview to call and check the status of the position.

Rule 2- Wait about two weeks and write a hand-written letter thanking them for the opportunity to have an interview with their company/organization. Also, use this time to reiterate your desire for the position. Obtain the address to their office and mail the letter.

Rule 3- Do not pester them by calling excessively. Your cover letter, resume, interview skills, and desire for the position will speak for itself.

Rule 4- If you are called in for a second and/or third interview, be sure to follow the dos and don'ts of the first interview. Sell yourself by letting the interviewer know **what you will do for their company/organization.**

*Ability is what you are capable of doing. Motivation determines what you do. Attitude determines how well you do it.*

– Lou Holtz

## From Me To You

*Hopefully, I have given you the insight and knowledge to successfully complete college. I can't guarantee that everything will be smooth sailing devoid of difficulty because it will not be. However, if you listen and execute the strategy that I have placed in front of you, you will do very well in college. Even after graduating, I can't guarantee that you will find a job quickly and without going that extra yard to obtain it. In our competitive global economy there are many educated and qualified potential candidates going for the same positions, but I have revealed information taken from firsthand experience on how to go about your job search. No matter how long it takes to finish, you will get there!!*

*Good luck, bonne chance, Удачи, Buena Suerta*

L.M. Bedell

P.S. The next few pages include advice given by students and professors on how to survive college.

# LEARNING FROM EXPERIENCE: TESTIMONIALS

**Here is what current and past students have to say...**

"Take college VERY seriously. Sacrifice everything you can while you are in college; trust me you will get rewarded in the long run. Manage your time wisely and DO NOT PROCRASTINATE! Keep your head held high even if you go through personal issues. Focus on what YOU want in life and if you go down the path you have created you WILL SUCCEED!"

"You are not like everyone else! We all have our own road to travel, sometimes we are alone and sometimes we get to enjoy company, but you rarely ever end up where you initially anticipated you would. Saying that to say this: what works for you may not work for the next one. It's always good to trust your instinct and go for what works for YOU, even if that means you have to be the odd man out. If life is becoming too intense, take a minute to be honest and truthful with yourself and recognize that. And if in that honesty you discover your priorities are not in order, either immediately place them there, or press pause to get it all together. The hardest part is being true to even yourself. People will always question you and give their opinions, but opinions are like food, take in what you can and save the rest for later otherwise you'll either be malnourished or overfed. Many think school is the best and sometimes only option one has in order to be successful. This is not necessarily so. Just look at those who didn't go to school yet have become influential to the world around us. Make your own path and don't be afraid to walk it alone if need be. School is not for everyone. Everyone will not survive. It is important to know where you stand and who you are. And it's not about not believing in yourself, it's about being wise and showing initiative and strength. It takes a lot for one to go against the grain, especially if he/she has ones around her counting on them. Just stay on YOUR path and don't be ashamed of YOUR journey."

"Don't start off at a big school; start at a small college and transfer to a bigger university."

"Don't succumb to peer pressure."

"It is good to be an idealist, but one should not forget about one's true self. There is no point in pretending that a student might stop having a social life if it is still going to play a big role. The most important thing is to learn how to plan a flexible schedule and TO PRIORITIZE. It is very important to try to get ahead before the classes begin. If possible, reading the syllabus and getting the books allows some students to begin and sometimes even complete some assignments before the semester even begins. Checking where each classroom is that way a student doesn't get lost or caught up trying to figure out how to get there when there is a crowd. Beware of one's personal weaknesses and strengths as it is good to learn to calculate how long and how much work it is going to take to complete an assignment, or to study for a test. It might create an imbalance in one's schedule when you need to complete too many assignments at once, or you have to study for several upcoming tests. Especially as a freshman, it can be a great tool for a student to join a freshman learning community, or another type of group where students that share a skill or interest can become supportive of each other besides classmates, but make sure that this or these groups have a well defined and productive goal besides socializing."

"Don't let yourself get in your own way."

"Make sure you are where you want to be, studying what you want to do. Have fun but not too much fun."

"Stay focused and don't let anything or no one distract you from what your goals are."

"Know how to control yourself and realize why you're doing this. Don't mess up because paying loans back is not fun. And do a study abroad."

"Get involved...do something more than just going to class. It makes you appreciate college more; if class is the only reason you are going to school, I think you are more likely to lose focus."

"Take advantage of the opportunities the school/environment provides you, because nowhere outside of college/university will you have those opportunities otherwise."

"90 percent of success is showing up to class."

"Know your purpose for attending college and have goals that you can constantly improve on or work towards, even if they're flexible. But if you don't have goals, be sure to continuously work on formulating those goals or at least know and have steps in place for success."

"Learn how to manage money and handle stress."

"Always get involved! Whether in an on-campus student organization or just in the classroom. Get to know your organization's advisor and professors. It makes it a lot easier when applying for jobs, internships, co-ops and even graduate or professional school."

"Every college student should have a 'plan b' to account for financial struggles and/or environmental disasters; self-evaluation is also important."

"At the end of every year or how often necessary one should take a step back and ask themselves important questions such as, What is my goal? What do I need to do in order to achieve my goal? Am I on track to achieving my goal? If one is satisfied with answers to the questions, that's awesome but if not, adjust your life accordingly. Be honest with yourself."

"Work first, play last, or play catch up later."

"Always step up and keep your options open because what you study might not necessarily be what you do. Follow your heart and not your wallet because the money will come."

"Would you pay for a Mercedes and not get leather? You're in school, now all you need to do is exploit your opportunity."

"Get all that you can from it. Learn to be versatile. Don't just study, don't just party; be well-rounded."

"Having a degree is highly overrated. It is going to take much more than graduation to ensure your success in life."

"Forget partying—try and stay focused during your first two years of school; know exactly what you want to study."

"Do not wait to the last minute to cram for exams. After every class, study the material you learned for at least thirty minutes; this will actually help you commit the information to memory."

"Enjoy the experience and take it as an opportunity to excel at whatever it is you want to do in life."

"Keep your options open while exploring different career fields and get as much out of class experience as possible."

"Always have an open mind; network throughout college."

"Take a couple classes that you may not want to take; this can open the door for new career opportunities."

"Save money in advance; learn to balance school, work, and social life. Don't let anything stress you out or overwhelm you."

"Time management is critical."

"Make school a primary not secondary priority."

"School is a process and is something that requires time and dedication. Thus, surround yourself with positive and proactive people. Set goals and push yourself to reach them. Develop relationships with other students and professors because they may be able to assist you with seeking employment after graduation."

"The key to success in college is finding the right balance between what you want to do and what you went there to do."

"Use weekend time wisely; use weekends to catch up on readings and other assignments."

"I have met some of my good friends while living on campus; stay on campus—it's a great experience."

"Forget how you studied in high school; College requires relentless studying so learn how to study properly."

"Don't be like me. Know exactly what you want to do with your life so take as many internships as possible. At least this will let you know what you don't want to do."

**Here is what professors have to say...**

"Go to class, do the reading, talk to the professors and other students and have fun with the materials and approach everything with an open but always skeptical mind."

"Wake up every morning assuming it'll be a good day—write down everything you need to do for the day, and then get the hardest/most stressful things done (or at least attempted) by 10 am. And always take lunch as time to relax and de-stress. Stress management is key to getting through school."

"Prepare for success in college by developing good study habits. Read as many books as possible, and turn off the TV!"

"Recognize that there are two (mostly) separate elements of the college experience, and students need to take both of them seriously. The first element is the classroom. By taking this seriously, I mean that the student should approach class work with the goal of learning something from those who are there to teach them, professors and other instructors. Know the syllabus, attend lecture, do the readings, study for tests, go to your professor's office hours—all to the larger goals of absorbing the lessons (both academic and otherwise) which are being taught. The second element is the social life. By taking this seriously, I mean take advantage of the opportunities afforded to you for friendships, activities, new experiences, and all the other wonderful opportunities college has to offer.

Students must strike a balance between both elements."

"The only good advice I have for you is to work hard and study, if you do these things, you will be successful."

"Do what makes your heart sing."

"Just keep working at it; I have one word for you 'PERSEVERANCE.'"

"Visit your professors on a regular basis."

"Take good notes; highlight what the professor repeats...9 times out 10 that information will be on the exam."

"Go the extra mile...determination will take you where hope can't go."

"Study like it's going out of style."

# REFERENCES

"College Student Debt Statistics." College Student
    Credit Card.
    http://www.collegestudentcreditcard.com/articles6.
    html.

"Proper Business Attire and Etiquette: Presenting the
    Complete Package." *TCB Solutions*.
    http://tcbsolutions.net/Proper_Attire_and_etiquet
    te_for_men_and_women.pdf.

"Students Become Prey for Cards Charging 18% After
    Free Lunch." *Bloomberg*.
    http://www.bloomberg.com/apps/news?pid=newsa
    rchive&sid=ajVskGdVyPSw.

"Why study abroad? 10 reasons why you should study in
    a foreign country." *Vistawide World Languages &
    Cultures*.

"Wisdom." Webster's New Notebook Dictionary. Def.
    1a-2. 2000.

Chu, Kathy. "Average college credit card debt rises with
    fees, tuition." *USATODAY on the Web*. (13 April
    2009). Accessed 31 August 2010.
    http://www.usatoday.com/money/perfi/2009-04-
    12-college-credit-card-debt_N.htm.

Delucchi, Michael. "Academic Performance in College
    Town." *Education, (1993)*: 114.1.

Harris-Bowlsbey, JoAnn. *Take Hold Of Your Future*. Iowa:
    Kuder, Inc, 2004.
    http://www.vistawide.com/studyabroad/year_of_st
    udy_abroad2006.htm.

Kimbrough, W and Hutcheson, P. "The Impact of
    Membership in Black Greek-Letter Organizations

on Black Students' Involvement in Collegiate Activities and Their Development of Leadership Skills." *Journal of Negro Education*, (1998): 67.2

Pike, Gary R. "The Influence of Fraternity or Sorority Membership on Students' College Experiences and Cognitive Development." *Research in Higher Education*, (2000): 41.1.

www.collegeboard.com

# ABOUT THE AUTHOR

L.M. Bedell was raised in Decatur, Georgia by hardworking parents that dreamed of her going to college. Her father always said that he wanted to live to see his daughter graduate from college—he was granted that wish before he died in February of 2011. She and her sister, Myecha Watkins, were the first to graduate college in their family despite facing family and economic instability. L.M. studied Political Science at Georgia State University where she graduated *magna cum laude* in December of 2009. She is currently songwriting and on a mission to help students achieve low stress and high grades.

### Contact Information:

www.collegecanbeasy.com

listentome1214@gmail.com

twitter.com/collegecanbeasy

facebook.com/collegecanbeasy

# NOTES

_____

_____

_____

_____

_____

_____

_____

_____

_____

_____

_____

_____

_____

_____